COUNTRY BIRD

Explore the Charming Language of Backcountry Birdsong

Angela Harrison Vinet
& Janis Hatten Harrison

EPIC INK

First published in 2024 by Epic Ink, an imprint of The Quarto Group,
142 West 36th Street, 4th Floor, New York, NY 10018, USA
T (212) 779-4972 www.Quarto.com

Epic Ink titles are also available at discount for retail, wholesale, promotional,
and bulk purchase. For details, contact the Special Sales Manager by
email at specialsales@quarto.com or by mail at The Quarto Group, Attn: Special
Sales Manager, 100 Cummings Center Suite 265D, Beverly, MA 01915 USA.

10 9 8 7 6 5 4 3 2 1

ISBN: 978-0-7603-8769-6

Digital edition published in 2024
eISBN: 978-0-7603-8770-2

Library of Congress Control Number: 2023945237

Group Publisher: Rage Kindelsperger
Creative Director: Laura Drew
Editorial Director: Lori Burke
Managing Editor: Cara Donaldson
Editor: Katie McGuire
Cover Design: Scott Richardson
Cover Illustration: Hannah George
Interior Design: Evelin Kasikov

Printed in China

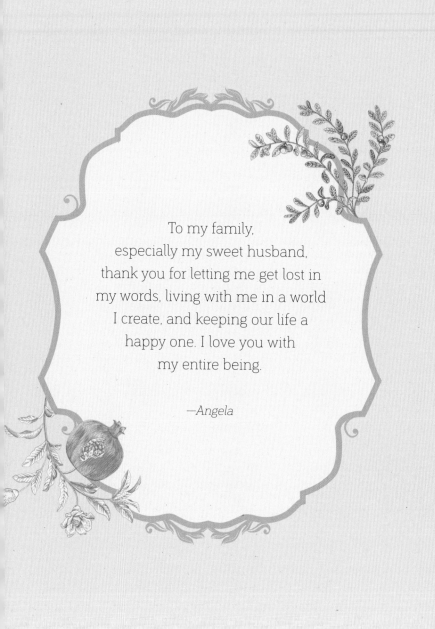

To my family,
especially my sweet husband,
thank you for letting me get lost in
my words, living with me in a world
I create, and keeping our life a
happy one. I love you with
my entire being.

—*Angela*

WELCOME, Y'ALL

This book is equally meant for the birds found in the countryside as for the bird-loving folk who live there or visit to admire their beauty and splendor. Within these pages you will discover a balance of words and illustrations intended to enrich a future bird outing, or to bring to the armchair birder a bewildering, feathery point of view inspired by the various regions where Country Birds can be found.

While some books give lessons on how to classify and label birds, this book will offer a pathway to become connected with birds through the sounds and songs heard on the farm and in the orchard. Not only do the following pages share a refreshing perspective on rural nature, but they also celebrate the whimsical traits and language of Country Birds that are amusing, relatable, and simply a hoot to observe.

COME SIT
A SPELL

Becoming a birder, while straightforward, is not without its rules of engagement. Let us be clear, anyone can become a passive spectator appreciating what our plumy friends have to offer, but if you want to truly experience the culture of birds and hold your own in the company of bird enthusiasts, there are three simple things to keep in mind:

NUMBER 1

Birds chirp, tweet, and sing—This language speaks to their actions and is the signal to help find them. Take in the chatter of Country Birds!

NUMBER 2

Be observant—The shapes, colors, and patterns of a Country Bird's plumage should be especially considered to ensure proper identification, from the dusty brown hue of the Barn Owl to the emerald-headed Mallard Duck.

NUMBER 3

Enjoy the view—Find a perch and watch the quirky, simple, and marvelous behaviors of Country Birds. Then you can speak with confidence (and a little swagger, too) about the nature of these extraordinary creatures.

The
Feathered
Country
Folk

···• Handier Than a Pocket on a Shirt •···

Keeping mice at bay, the Barn Owl
is a farmer's best friend. It is both a master
of pest control and a useful watchful eye,
so scurrying mice stand very little chance
against a Barn Owl's ambush, experiencing
a quick death by being swallowed whole by
this Country Bird. A "Night Owl" indeed, this
nocturnal hunter ambushes unsuspecting prey
from a perfectly camouflaged perch. If you
happen upon a large, oblong ball, make sure
to examine the contents, as it is likely a Barn
Owl's pellet; these stunning, savage hunters
spit out the hair and bones of the small
mammals they devour like a cat coughing up a
hairball. Of all the owls in the family, the Barn
Owl is a slender beauty with its trademark
long legs that are certain to catch a second
glance when its feathered skirt is lifted.

···· Birds of a Feather Dance Together ····

Watching a *kettle* of Swallows dance
at dusk as they gobble up pesky insects is
simply delightful. This Country Bird is sleek
and sophisticated, with gorgeous top feathers
so black they're blue, and rusty-rose down
feathers accented by a deeply forked tail with
a white semicircle trim. Lady Barn Swallows
appreciate a great tail piece and choose their
mates according to tail length. *Some* folks may
regard this Country Bird's unique mud nest
as a nuisance, but that's just too darn bad—
Barn Swallows are protected by the Migratory
Bird Treaty Act of 1918. And thanks to these
birds' dexterity, mosquitos don't stand a
chance when a Barn Swallow is
soaring through the field.

···• A Feathery Bandit •···

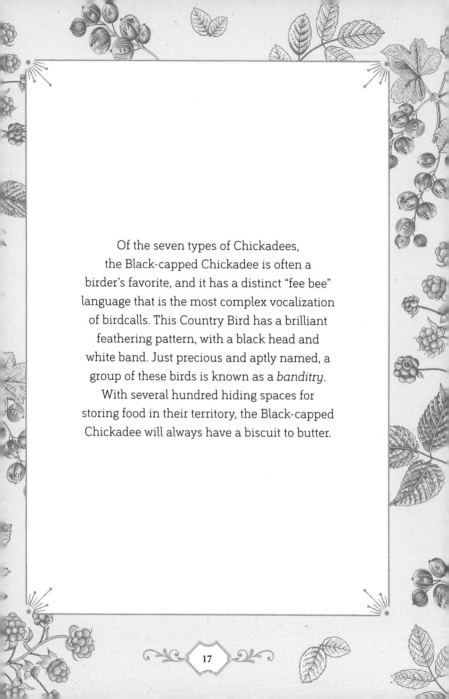

Of the seven types of Chickadees,
the Black-capped Chickadee is often a
birder's favorite, and it has a distinct "fee bee"
language that is the most complex vocalization
of birdcalls. This Country Bird has a brilliant
feathering pattern, with a black head and
white band. Just precious and aptly named, a
group of these birds is known as a *banditry*.
With several hundred hiding spaces for
storing food in their territory, the Black-capped
Chickadee will always have a biscuit to butter.

··→ A Westward Wanderer ←··

When homes began to be built on prairie land in the western part of North America, this Country Bird spread its wings and headed west! One of the few birds that can safely eat a poisonous monarch butterfly, the Black-headed Grosbeak, with its orange body and black wings, looks like the prey it devours.

···• Madder Than a Wet Hen •···

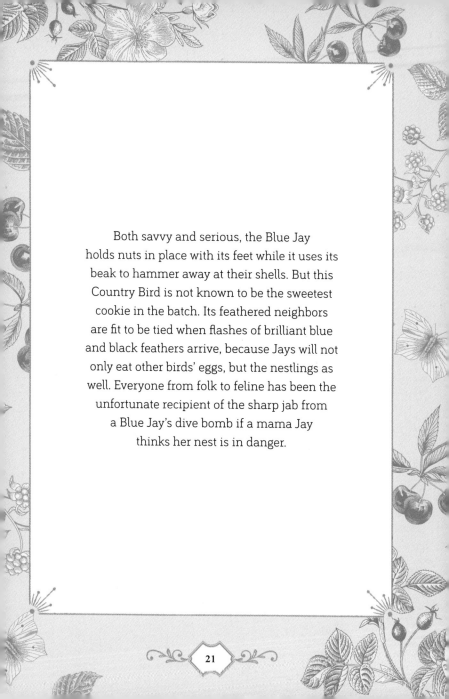

Both savvy and serious, the Blue Jay holds nuts in place with its feet while it uses its beak to hammer away at their shells. But this Country Bird is not known to be the sweetest cookie in the batch. Its feathered neighbors are fit to be tied when flashes of brilliant blue and black feathers arrive, because Jays will not only eat other birds' eggs, but the nestlings as well. Everyone from folk to feline has been the unfortunate recipient of the sharp jab from a Blue Jay's dive bomb if a mama Jay thinks her nest is in danger.

··· Flimflammer ···

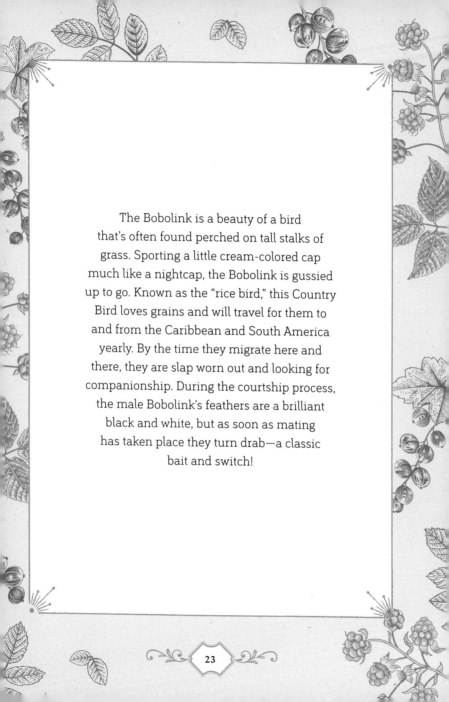

The Bobolink is a beauty of a bird
that's often found perched on tall stalks of
grass. Sporting a little cream-colored cap
much like a nightcap, the Bobolink is gussied
up to go. Known as the "rice bird," this Country
Bird loves grains and will travel for them to
and from the Caribbean and South America
yearly. By the time they migrate here and
there, they are slap worn out and looking for
companionship. During the courtship process,
the male Bobolink's feathers are a brilliant
black and white, but as soon as mating
has taken place they turn drab—a classic
bait and switch!

THE BREWER'S BLACKBIRD

···▶ Wearin' Out Yer Welcome ◀···

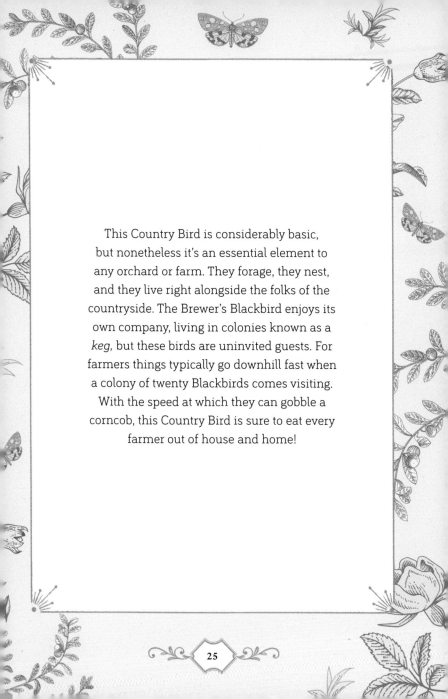

This Country Bird is considerably basic,
but nonetheless it's an essential element to
any orchard or farm. They forage, they nest,
and they live right alongside the folks of the
countryside. The Brewer's Blackbird enjoys its
own company, living in colonies known as a
keg, but these birds are uninvited guests. For
farmers things typically go downhill fast when
a colony of twenty Blackbirds comes visiting.
With the speed at which they can gobble a
corncob, this Country Bird is sure to eat every
farmer out of house and home!

THE BROWN CREEPER

·••· Busy as a Cat on a Hot Tin Roof ·••·

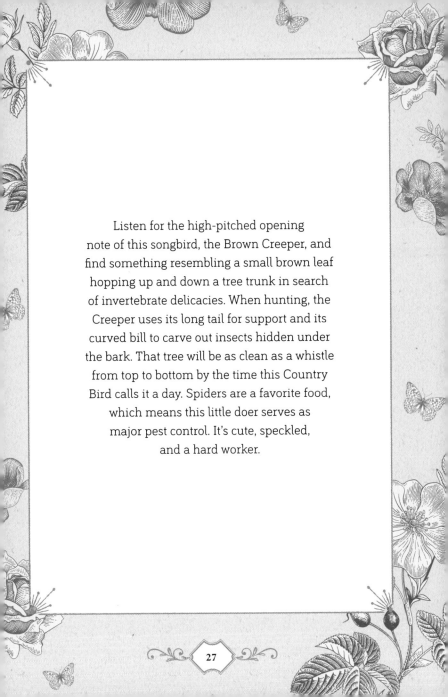

Listen for the high-pitched opening
note of this songbird, the Brown Creeper, and
find something resembling a small brown leaf
hopping up and down a tree trunk in search
of invertebrate delicacies. When hunting, the
Creeper uses its long tail for support and its
curved bill to carve out insects hidden under
the bark. That tree will be as clean as a whistle
from top to bottom by the time this Country
Bird calls it a day. Spiders are a favorite food,
which means this little doer serves as
major pest control. It's cute, speckled,
and a hard worker.

···• Watch Out or I'll Cream Yer Corn •···

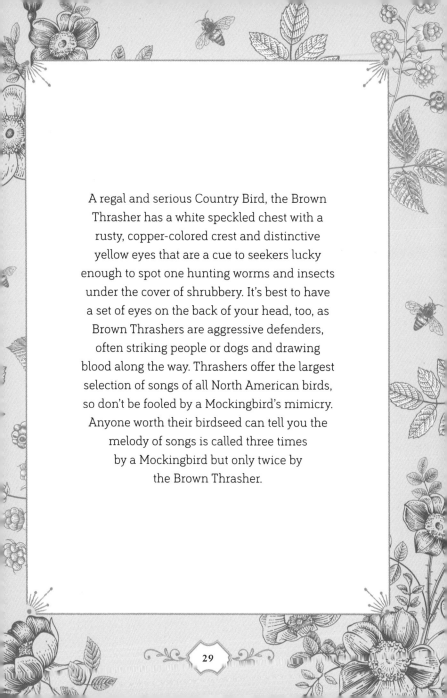

A regal and serious Country Bird, the Brown Thrasher has a white speckled chest with a rusty, copper-colored crest and distinctive yellow eyes that are a cue to seekers lucky enough to spot one hunting worms and insects under the cover of shrubbery. It's best to have a set of eyes on the back of your head, too, as Brown Thrashers are aggressive defenders, often striking people or dogs and drawing blood along the way. Thrashers offer the largest selection of songs of all North American birds, so don't be fooled by a Mockingbird's mimicry. Anyone worth their birdseed can tell you the melody of songs is called three times by a Mockingbird but only twice by the Brown Thrasher.

···• Many Hands Make Light Work •···

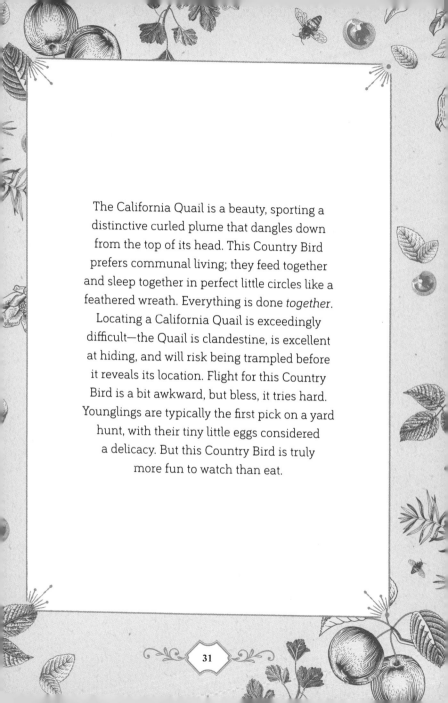

The California Quail is a beauty, sporting a distinctive curled plume that dangles down from the top of its head. This Country Bird prefers communal living; they feed together and sleep together in perfect little circles like a feathered wreath. Everything is done *together*. Locating a California Quail is exceedingly difficult—the Quail is clandestine, is excellent at hiding, and will risk being trampled before it reveals its location. Flight for this Country Bird is a bit awkward, but bless, it tries hard. Younglings are typically the first pick on a yard hunt, with their tiny little eggs considered a delicacy. But this Country Bird is truly more fun to watch than eat.

···• Birdie in Red •···

The Cardinal, known as the "Red Bird," is nothing short of majestic and heavenly. These Country Birds daringly fly and dash from bush to tree in flashes of radiant red, aggressively defending their territory in mating season but singing as sweet as pie once the hormones subside. Cardinals are a favorite when visiting the countryside—a comforting old adage entertained by many is that when a red bird is sighted, it symbolizes a visit from a loved one who has passed.

···• Whiskey in a Teacup •···

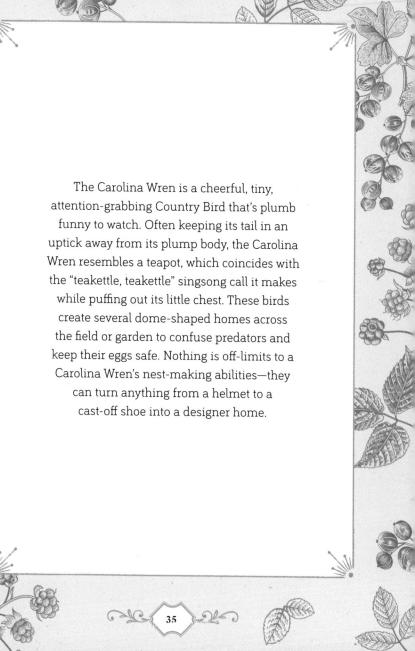

The Carolina Wren is a cheerful, tiny, attention-grabbing Country Bird that's plumb funny to watch. Often keeping its tail in an uptick away from its plump body, the Carolina Wren resembles a teapot, which coincides with the "teakettle, teakettle" singsong call it makes while puffing out its little chest. These birds create several dome-shaped homes across the field or garden to confuse predators and keep their eggs safe. Nothing is off-limits to a Carolina Wren's nest-making abilities—they can turn anything from a helmet to a cast-off shoe into a designer home.

···• Knee-high to a Grasshopper •···

The Chipping Sparrow is easily identified by the quintessential rusty red cap on its crown. The tiniest of Sparrows and fairly common, this Country Bird can be found hopping in grasses or gobbling up goodies found in the dirt. Their song is more like one continuous chirp, almost cricket-like, which folks might mistake for that of an insect. Chipping Sparrows lay beautiful blue eggs that are sometimes speckled. To incubate the eggs, mama Sparrows will shed feathers on an area of her belly called a *brood patch*, which will keep the eggs warmer. The nests are easily seen, positioned low in shrubs or tree branches with such loose construction that it's almost a danger zone. Heavens to Betsy, it's a miracle the babies don't fall out!

···• What in the Sam Hill is That? •···

The Common Nighthawk could fool folks and farmers with its name alone. This bird is not nocturnal, nor related to a Hawk. Often confused with a bat due to its erratic flight path, which is indeed "batty," this gorgeous Country Bird devours massive amounts of mosquitos, just like its flying mammal friend. The Common Nighthawk is active at both dawn and dusk hunting insects, especially around tall lights and treetops. As gravel nesters the parents are solitary, but as soon as the young ones are out of the house these birds take a destination-unknown vacation. No one seems to know where these birds migrate to, but who could fault them? If the striking white stripes on the wings aren't a giveaway, the booming and zooming sound they make while in motion, like a jet plane flyby, lets folks know the Common Nighthawk is around.

···› Jesus, Take the Wheel ‹···

High-speed chases, crashes through foliage, and certain death may sound like an exhilarating film, but this action scene is performed in the great outdoors by none other than the Cooper's Hawk. Similar in build to a Falcon, the Cooper's Hawk appears as a cross when soaring because of the silhouette it makes against the sky. But Jesus takes the wheel when this bird comes a-callin'! The great white shark of the bird world, the Cooper's Hawk is gorgeous but dangerous. Feeding mostly on other birds and small mammals, a Cooper's Hawk attacks at such high speed and so viciously that the prey often suffers a broken wishbone. Their dinner choice can also be drowned or squeezed to death by the talons of the Cooper's Hawk. Returning to the same nest year after year, this Country Bird predator announces its arrival with piercing birdcall vocalizations.

···→ A Real Snake in the Grass ←···

This pickpocket of a Country Bird is an opportunist for a fast bite to eat and is rarely particular about what is on the menu. Nothing is off-limits for this bird's palate—ranging from plant-based meals to even the dead, which will suffice when that's in reach of the Crow's claw. Crafty and smart, with long memories and lifespans, we see scarecrows go up in gardens and fields to trick and defend against a murder of Crows looking for an early harvest feasting. The whole bird community gets fussy and throws a hissy when these swindlers swoop into town; they are known to snatch up the younglings for a quick meal, causing complete birdie chaos.

THE CURVE-BILLED THRASHER

···• Raising Them Right •···

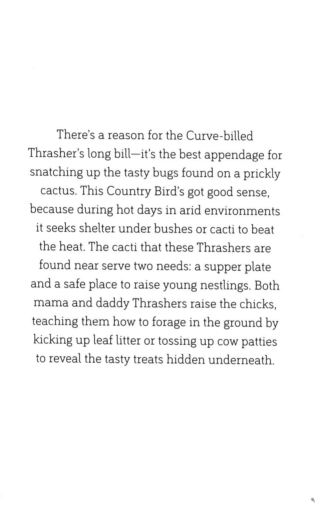

There's a reason for the Curve-billed Thrasher's long bill—it's the best appendage for snatching up the tasty bugs found on a prickly cactus. This Country Bird's got good sense, because during hot days in arid environments it seeks shelter under bushes or cacti to beat the heat. The cacti that these Thrashers are found near serve two needs: a supper plate and a safe place to raise young nestlings. Both mama and daddy Thrashers raise the chicks, teaching them how to forage in the ground by kicking up leaf litter or tossing up cow patties to reveal the tasty treats hidden underneath.

··· Making Some Noise ···

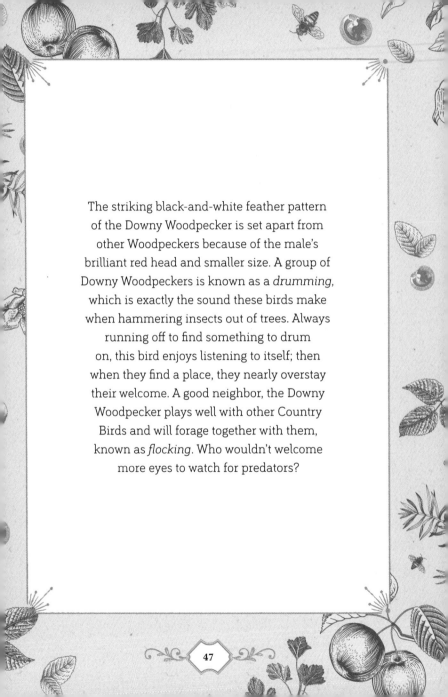

The striking black-and-white feather pattern of the Downy Woodpecker is set apart from other Woodpeckers because of the male's brilliant red head and smaller size. A group of Downy Woodpeckers is known as a *drumming,* which is exactly the sound these birds make when hammering insects out of trees. Always running off to find something to drum on, this bird enjoys listening to itself; then when they find a place, they nearly overstay their welcome. A good neighbor, the Downy Woodpecker plays well with other Country Birds and will forage together with them, known as *flocking.* Who wouldn't welcome more eyes to watch for predators?

···• Tickle Your Fancy •···

Taking a drive down the dusty dirt road of the countryside will sure as Christmas give you a glimpse of the Eastern Bluebird. In true natural world fashion, the males have the brilliant coloring of a bright-blue back and rusty-red chest, while the females are color conservative and a bit drab. These Country Birds seem to skedaddle and never sit too long on the fence post. Like a ray of sunshine with wings, Eastern Bluebirds are bearers of joy and happiness, especially when they are seen in the wild.

···• Spittin' in the Punch Bowl •···

The Eastern Screech Owl patiently waits on unsuspecting prey, perfectly camouflaged against the bark and lichen within which it conceals itself. While pairs mate for life, the Eastern Screech Owl male has a wandering eye. Although he sometimes mates with two females, the newer bird will look to evict the original, raising quite the ruckus. Listen for a spooky call, and that would be the Eastern Screech Owl. Folks are made aware of this Country Bird's presence long before seeing or hearing one because the bird chatter goes suddenly quiet. It's all fun and games until the Screech Owl shows up to spoil the party.

···→ Miss Highfalutin ←···

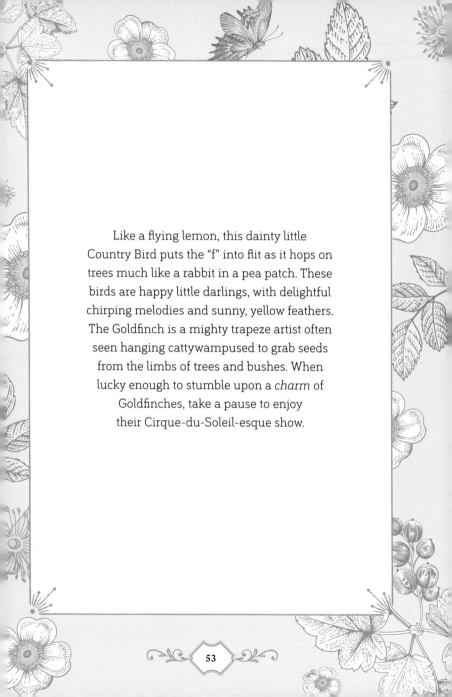

Like a flying lemon, this dainty little Country Bird puts the "f" into flit as it hops on trees much like a rabbit in a pea patch. These birds are happy little darlings, with delightful chirping melodies and sunny, yellow feathers. The Goldfinch is a mighty trapeze artist often seen hanging cattywampused to grab seeds from the limbs of trees and bushes. When lucky enough to stumble upon a *charm* of Goldfinches, take a pause to enjoy their Cirque-du-Soleil-esque show.

···• Come on in—and Stay Awhile •···

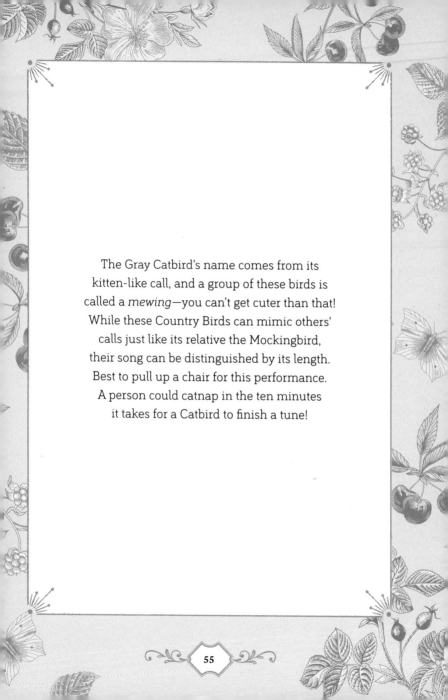

The Gray Catbird's name comes from its
kitten-like call, and a group of these birds is
called a *mewing*—you can't get cuter than that!
While these Country Birds can mimic others'
calls just like its relative the Mockingbird,
their song can be distinguished by its length.
Best to pull up a chair for this performance.
A person could catnap in the ten minutes
it takes for a Catbird to finish a tune!

GREAT BLUE HERON

···• The Steel Magnolia •···

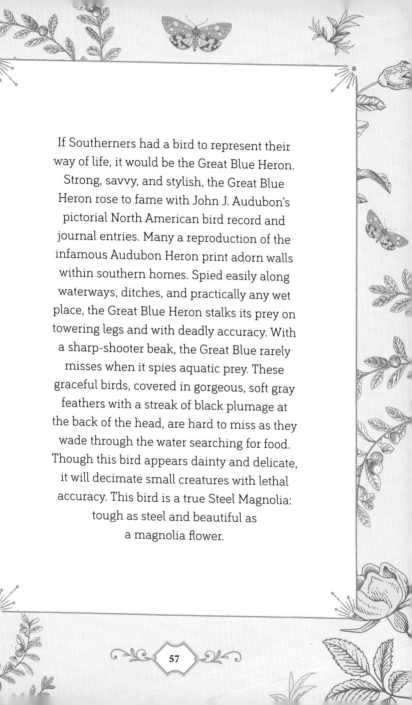

If Southerners had a bird to represent their way of life, it would be the Great Blue Heron. Strong, savvy, and stylish, the Great Blue Heron rose to fame with John J. Audubon's pictorial North American bird record and journal entries. Many a reproduction of the infamous Audubon Heron print adorn walls within southern homes. Spied easily along waterways, ditches, and practically any wet place, the Great Blue Heron stalks its prey on towering legs and with deadly accuracy. With a sharp-shooter beak, the Great Blue rarely misses when it spies aquatic prey. These graceful birds, covered in gorgeous, soft gray feathers with a streak of black plumage at the back of the head, are hard to miss as they wade through the water searching for food. Though this bird appears dainty and delicate, it will decimate small creatures with lethal accuracy. This bird is a true Steel Magnolia: tough as steel and beautiful as a magnolia flower.

···• Useful as a Tit on a Boar Hog •···

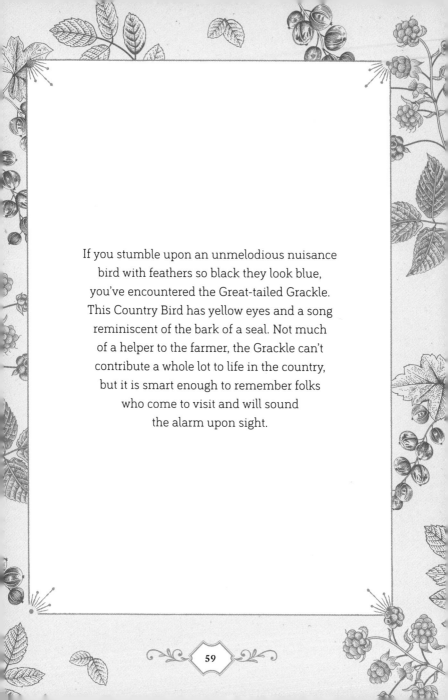

If you stumble upon an unmelodious nuisance
bird with feathers so black they look blue,
you've encountered the Great-tailed Grackle.
This Country Bird has yellow eyes and a song
reminiscent of the bark of a seal. Not much
of a helper to the farmer, the Grackle can't
contribute a whole lot to life in the country,
but it is smart enough to remember folks
who come to visit and will sound
the alarm upon sight.

THE HORNED LARK

•••• Setting Up Home Sweet Home ••••

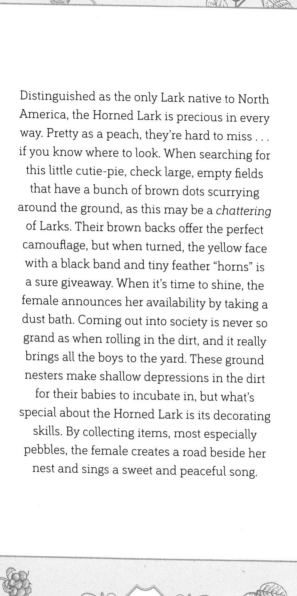

Distinguished as the only Lark native to North America, the Horned Lark is precious in every way. Pretty as a peach, they're hard to miss . . . if you know where to look. When searching for this little cutie-pie, check large, empty fields that have a bunch of brown dots scurrying around the ground, as this may be a *chattering* of Larks. Their brown backs offer the perfect camouflage, but when turned, the yellow face with a black band and tiny feather "horns" is a sure giveaway. When it's time to shine, the female announces her availability by taking a dust bath. Coming out into society is never so grand as when rolling in the dirt, and it really brings all the boys to the yard. These ground nesters make shallow depressions in the dirt for their babies to incubate in, but what's special about the Horned Lark is its decorating skills. By collecting items, most especially pebbles, the female creates a road beside her nest and sings a sweet and peaceful song.

···· Just as Fancy as Granny's Lace ····

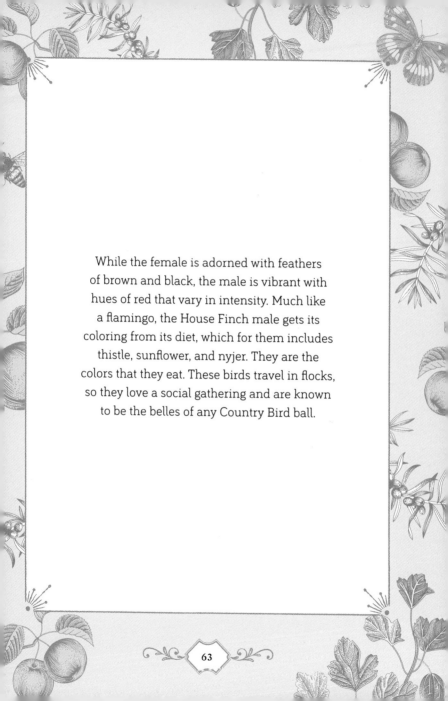

While the female is adorned with feathers of brown and black, the male is vibrant with hues of red that vary in intensity. Much like a flamingo, the House Finch male gets its coloring from its diet, which for them includes thistle, sunflower, and nyjer. They are the colors that they eat. These birds travel in flocks, so they love a social gathering and are known to be the belles of any Country Bird ball.

···• Too Big for its Britches •···

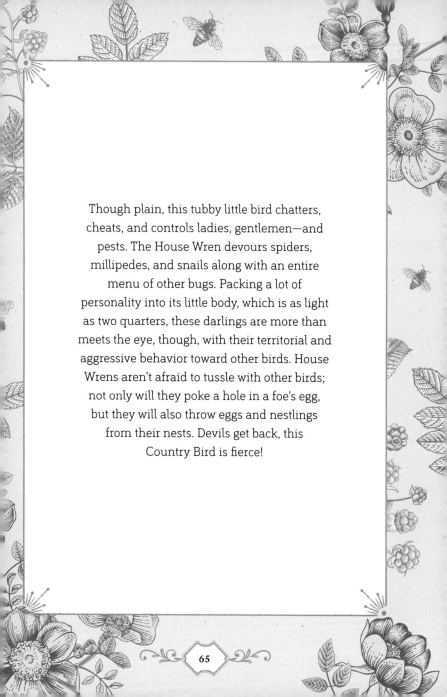

Though plain, this tubby little bird chatters, cheats, and controls ladies, gentlemen—and pests. The House Wren devours spiders, millipedes, and snails along with an entire menu of other bugs. Packing a lot of personality into its little body, which is as light as two quarters, these darlings are more than meets the eye, though, with their territorial and aggressive behavior toward other birds. House Wrens aren't afraid to tussle with other birds; not only will they poke a hole in a foe's egg, but they will also throw eggs and nestlings from their nests. Devils get back, this Country Bird is fierce!

···· Phony Baloney ····

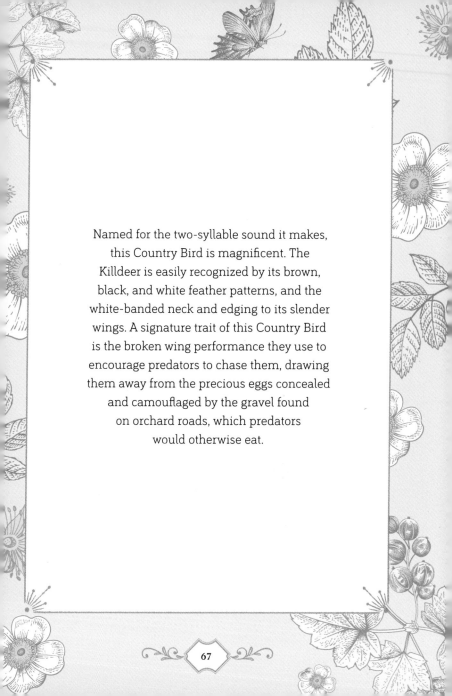

Named for the two-syllable sound it makes, this Country Bird is magnificent. The Killdeer is easily recognized by its brown, black, and white feather patterns, and the white-banded neck and edging to its slender wings. A signature trait of this Country Bird is the broken wing performance they use to encourage predators to chase them, drawing them away from the precious eggs concealed and camouflaged by the gravel found on orchard roads, which predators would otherwise eat.

···· Practice Makes Perfect ····

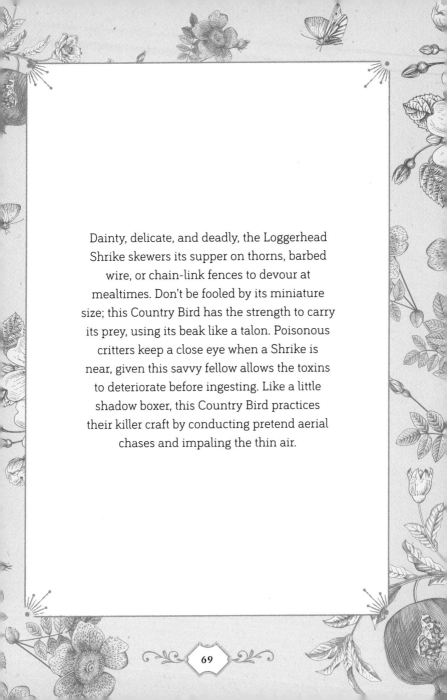

Dainty, delicate, and deadly, the Loggerhead Shrike skewers its supper on thorns, barbed wire, or chain-link fences to devour at mealtimes. Don't be fooled by its miniature size; this Country Bird has the strength to carry its prey, using its beak like a talon. Poisonous critters keep a close eye when a Shrike is near, given this savvy fellow allows the toxins to deteriorate before ingesting. Like a little shadow boxer, this Country Bird practices their killer craft by conducting pretend aerial chases and impaling the thin air.

THE MOURNING DOVE

···• Sure to Pepper the Gumbo •···

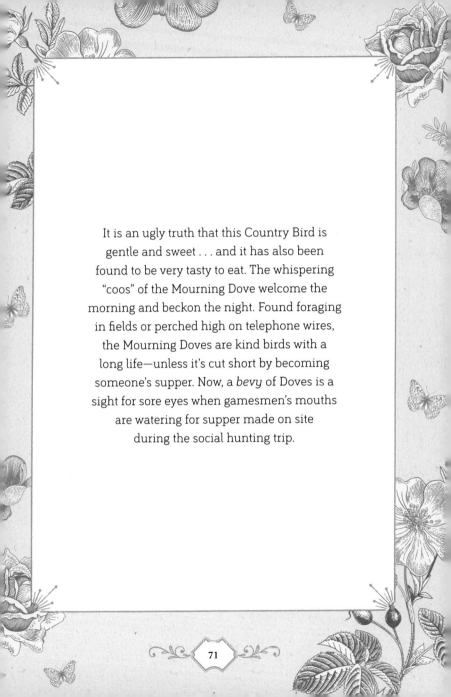

It is an ugly truth that this Country Bird is gentle and sweet . . . and it has also been found to be very tasty to eat. The whispering "coos" of the Mourning Dove welcome the morning and beckon the night. Found foraging in fields or perched high on telephone wires, the Mourning Doves are kind birds with a long life—unless it's cut short by becoming someone's supper. Now, a *bevy* of Doves is a sight for sore eyes when gamesmen's mouths are watering for supper made on site during the social hunting trip.

THE NORTHERN FLICKER

--- Howdy Y'all ---

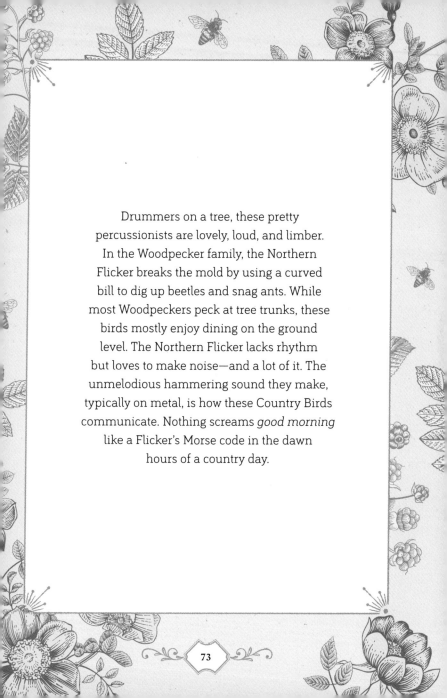

Drummers on a tree, these pretty percussionists are lovely, loud, and limber. In the Woodpecker family, the Northern Flicker breaks the mold by using a curved bill to dig up beetles and snag ants. While most Woodpeckers peck at tree trunks, these birds mostly enjoy dining on the ground level. The Northern Flicker lacks rhythm but loves to make noise—and a lot of it. The unmelodious hammering sound they make, typically on metal, is how these Country Birds communicate. Nothing screams *good morning* like a Flicker's Morse code in the dawn hours of a country day.

···• Sassy Sassafras •···

The Northern Mockingbird is one of the most musical and complex singers in the bird world. It was just born that way. In fact, it is so respected that in the early 1800s in America people would take nestlings and keep them in cages, then sell them to collectors, which would fetch large sums of money—especially the most talented singing birds. Endlessly stringing together other birds' songs, the Northern Mockingbird is the ultimate plagiarizer. This Country Bird is a rather grumpy fowl and doesn't play or share well with others. Best to stay in the balcony seats and enjoy this musical maestro from afar.

THE PURPLE MARTIN

···• It's Got Good Horse Sense •···

More than meets the eye, Purple Martins are apartment nesters living in a bonded colony and chatting up the neighbors. Coming back to the same home every year, the Purple Martin sends scouts ahead of the colony to inspect the nesting site. Feeding and drinking in flight, these Country Birds are aerial acrobats that make unmistakable sounds. They'll be cattywampus in the sky catching bugs and they have good horse sense for a bird! Contrary to widely held belief, these little stinkers don't eat mosquitoes, they actually eat the insects that eat mosquitoes, such as dragonflies or mosquito hawks.

···→ Blowin' Up a Storm ←···

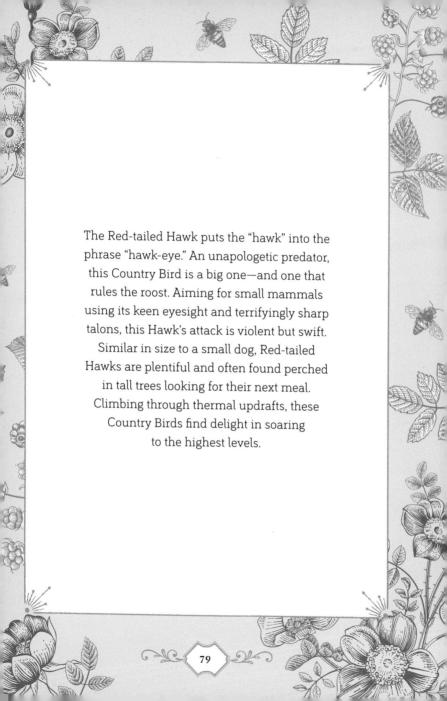

The Red-tailed Hawk puts the "hawk" into the phrase "hawk-eye." An unapologetic predator, this Country Bird is a big one—and one that rules the roost. Aiming for small mammals using its keen eyesight and terrifyingly sharp talons, this Hawk's attack is violent but swift.

Similar in size to a small dog, Red-tailed Hawks are plentiful and often found perched in tall trees looking for their next meal. Climbing through thermal updrafts, these Country Birds find delight in soaring to the highest levels.

···· Just Hunky-dory ····

It's hard to miss the male Red-winged Blackbird, with its sleek black body and striking epaulets of red and gold. This Country Bird is so purdy. In true bird fashion, the female is camouflaged like the colors of her nest, while the male is simply stunning. Abundant and bold, these birds are an unwelcome guest at a group foraging. Like a flying pig, it'll eat up everything in sight, lickety-split. In the country, they can be found perched on cattails or on the stalks of tall grasses. These birds will nest just about anywhere, but they are as snug as bugs in marshy areas. The vivid markings are a dead giveaway, along with the "okalee" song they sing.

··· Game Recognizes Game ···

The Ring-necked Pheasant is a popular game bird, but it's stunning both off and on the dinner table. Striking in appearance, with shimmering copper coloring, a bluish-green hood, and a bold white band around the neck, it's a beaut. Neither a songbird nor a migratory bird, this Country Bird is "fair game" and, therefore, exempt from the Migratory Bird Treaty Act for hunting.

···• Busier Than a Bee in a Tar Bucket •···

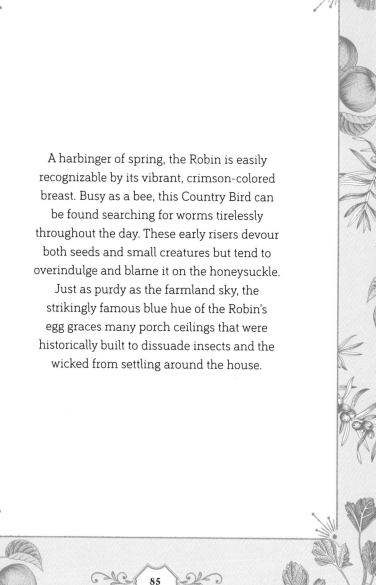

A harbinger of spring, the Robin is easily recognizable by its vibrant, crimson-colored breast. Busy as a bee, this Country Bird can be found searching for worms tirelessly throughout the day. These early risers devour both seeds and small creatures but tend to overindulge and blame it on the honeysuckle. Just as purdy as the farmland sky, the strikingly famous blue hue of the Robin's egg graces many porch ceilings that were historically built to dissuade insects and the wicked from settling around the house.

ROSEATE SPOONBILL

···• It'll Knock Your Socks Off •···

With their spoon-shaped bills and looking like a bird out of a fantasy novel, the Roseate Spoonbill will have bird-watchers doing a double take. Reminiscent of a Lewis Carroll character from *Alice in Wonderland,* this water bird is pinky-pink, thanks to a diet consisting of their favorite crustaceans and invertebrates. Rhythmically sweeping the water's bottom, Spoonbills will become more vibrantly pink with each nibble. These birds also offer beauty in numbers, as they enjoy the company of other waterfowl. Ibis, Blue Herons, Egrets, and Spoonbills often feed together, in a gorgeous display of birds. Spoonbills gift their mates hand-selected sticks, and pairs can be found in trees by the water's edge, in nests built with these fancy stick gifts. The only drawback to being a Spoonbill is the hair loss. As they age, bless their hearts, these poor things go bald!

···• Reckon It's Dead? •···

Do not be alarmed when stumbling upon this Country Bird in the wild; the red splash of coloring on its throat and chest is a characteristic feature of the Rose-breasted Grosbeak—it is not hurt. While these birds migrate through the countryside of many Southern states, they actually prefer the Northern climates. Digesting insects, seeds, and berries, they find their dinner plate within shrubs and trees. The melody of the Rose-breasted Grosbeak is similar to that of a Robin, yet different, with a richer, more polished tune.

···➤ Pretty as a Peach ◄···

The Ruby-crowned Kinglet is a tiny bird that flickers its wings wildly while showing off that stunning, olive-green coloring and those fancy black and gray wing bars. Though they're only as heavy as a quarter, don't let the size fool you, because this Country Bird can lay as many as twelve eggs (yes, a full dozen!) in a single batch. As an acrobatic forager, these nervous Nellies dine on aphids, caterpillars, and other insects. The Ruby-crowned Kinglet's constant movement is spent finding food or lining cute nests with soft mosses and lichens. The most adorable aspect of this feathered friend is his red mohawk safely tucked back until provoked. Though it's pretty as a peach, beware this feathered friend's temper—that mohawk will fly when agitated.

THE RUDDY DUCK

··· Fussy Feathers ···

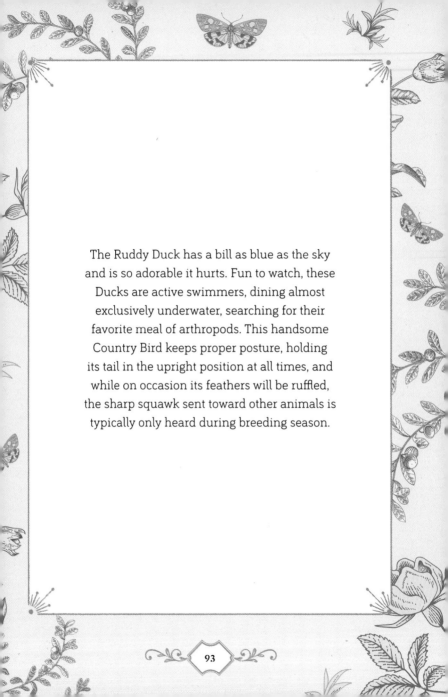

The Ruddy Duck has a bill as blue as the sky and is so adorable it hurts. Fun to watch, these Ducks are active swimmers, dining almost exclusively underwater, searching for their favorite meal of arthropods. This handsome Country Bird keeps proper posture, holding its tail in the upright position at all times, and while on occasion its feathers will be ruffled, the sharp squawk sent toward other animals is typically only heard during breeding season.

···· Quite a Looker ····

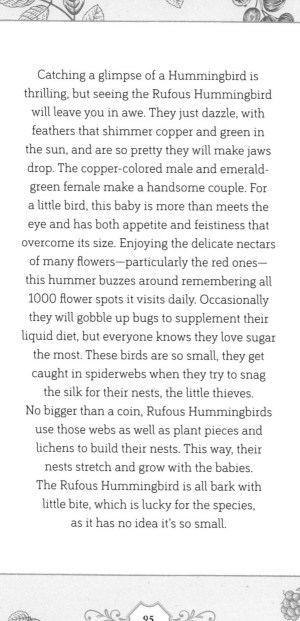

Catching a glimpse of a Hummingbird is
thrilling, but seeing the Rufous Hummingbird
will leave you in awe. They just dazzle, with
feathers that shimmer copper and green in
the sun, and are so pretty they will make jaws
drop. The copper-colored male and emerald-
green female make a handsome couple. For
a little bird, this baby is more than meets the
eye and has both appetite and feistiness that
overcome its size. Enjoying the delicate nectars
of many flowers—particularly the red ones—
this hummer buzzes around remembering all
1000 flower spots it visits daily. Occasionally
they will gobble up bugs to supplement their
liquid diet, but everyone knows they love sugar
the most. These birds are so small, they get
caught in spiderwebs when they try to snag
the silk for their nests, the little thieves.
No bigger than a coin, Rufous Hummingbirds
use those webs as well as plant pieces and
lichens to build their nests. This way, their
nests stretch and grow with the babies.
The Rufous Hummingbird is all bark with
little bite, which is lucky for the species,
as it has no idea it's so small.

THE SONG SPARROW

⤙⤙ Sings Like an Angel ⤚⤚

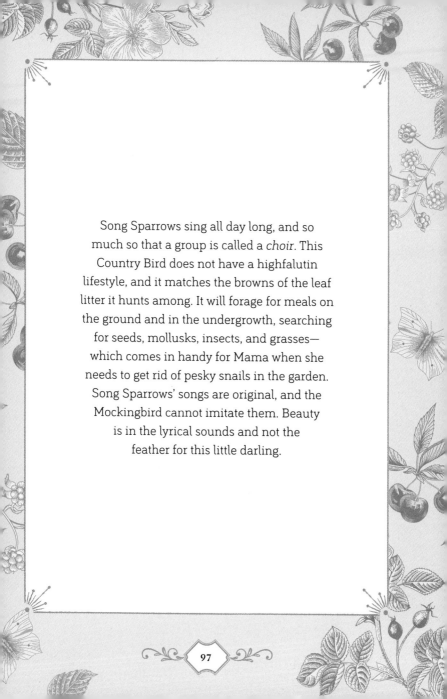

Song Sparrows sing all day long, and so much so that a group is called a *choir*. This Country Bird does not have a highfalutin lifestyle, and it matches the browns of the leaf litter it hunts among. It will forage for meals on the ground and in the undergrowth, searching for seeds, mollusks, insects, and grasses— which comes in handy for Mama when she needs to get rid of pesky snails in the garden. Song Sparrows' songs are original, and the Mockingbird cannot imitate them. Beauty is in the lyrical sounds and not the feather for this little darling.

THE WESTERN KINGBIRD

···• That Bird's Got Gumption •···

A fierce flycatcher, the Western Kingbird should come with a warning label to those looking to provoke its nest. As the royalty of the bird world, it offers displays of aerial dominance, like an airshow for birds. The male Western Kingbird will twist and turn, stall, and fall to flex his wings. This is one show everyone will pull the lawn chairs out to watch. Those flying skills come in handy when catching buzzing insects on the move for their favorite meal. Recognizable by their sunny yellow chest and gray back, the Western Kingbird can be found from coast to coast hunting prey and eating berries. Large birds do not frighten these fierce, feathered friends. Let me tell you, they aggressively defend their territory from any predator with harsh flybys. Don't poke this Country Bird or the red feathers hidden under the crown will appear!

···•··· Two-timer ···•···

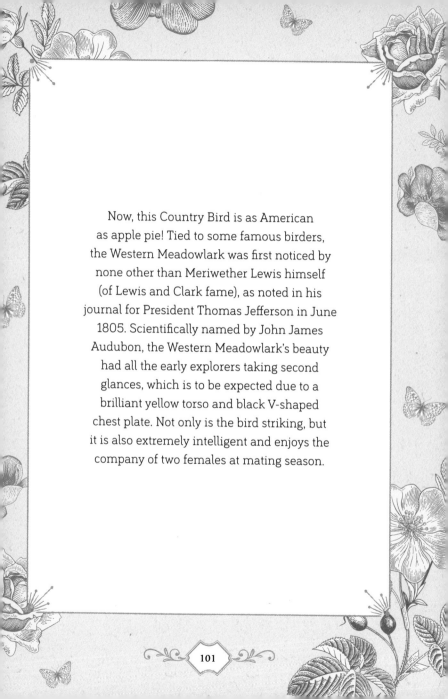

Now, this Country Bird is as American as apple pie! Tied to some famous birders, the Western Meadowlark was first noticed by none other than Meriwether Lewis himself (of Lewis and Clark fame), as noted in his journal for President Thomas Jefferson in June 1805. Scientifically named by John James Audubon, the Western Meadowlark's beauty had all the early explorers taking second glances, which is to be expected due to a brilliant yellow torso and black V-shaped chest plate. Not only is the bird striking, but it is also extremely intelligent and enjoys the company of two females at mating season.

···▸ A Social Butterfly ◂···

This Country Bird appears dressed for dinner, with a more distinguished look than its relatives. Contrasting white and gray feather patterns are highlighted with black-trimmed accent feathers that create a sharp tuxedo look. This type of Nuthatch lives year-round in the same spot, which makes for predictable bird-watching, but it's still a sight worth seeing.

···• Mind Yer Elders •···

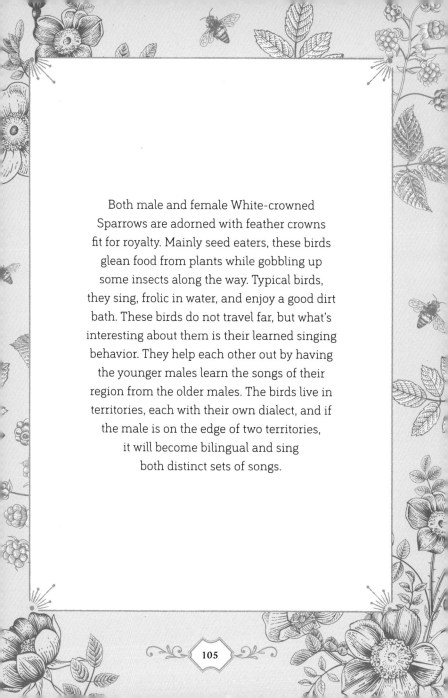

Both male and female White-crowned Sparrows are adorned with feather crowns fit for royalty. Mainly seed eaters, these birds glean food from plants while gobbling up some insects along the way. Typical birds, they sing, frolic in water, and enjoy a good dirt bath. These birds do not travel far, but what's interesting about them is their learned singing behavior. They help each other out by having the younger males learn the songs of their region from the older males. The birds live in territories, each with their own dialect, and if the male is on the edge of two territories, it will become bilingual and sing both distinct sets of songs.

THE WILD TURKEY

···· Gobble with a Wobble ····

Most widely known for gracing the dinner table at Thanksgiving, this Country Bird is more than a meal. These domesticated birds are native to North America, thriving on acorns while wandering forests and clearings. When the distinctive "gobble" of the Wild Turkey is heard, look for a whole posse of hens with their broods. The ladies like to raise their chicks together. Males on a mission for a mate will display their spectacular tail fans and fluff themselves into balls of feathers, with layers upon layers of rich feather patterns. Talk 'bout shaking a tail feather—a full display draws the ladies in like nectar does a bee. The Wild Turkey is as delightful a sight in the wild as it is delicious.

···• Like a Starving Man on a Country Ham •···

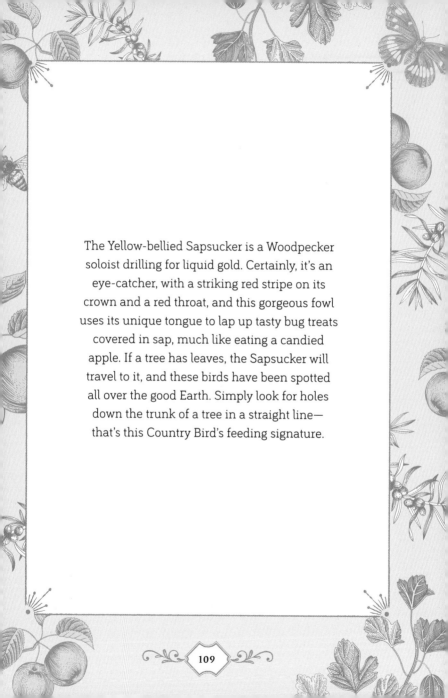

The Yellow-bellied Sapsucker is a Woodpecker soloist drilling for liquid gold. Certainly, it's an eye-catcher, with a striking red stripe on its crown and a red throat, and this gorgeous fowl uses its unique tongue to lap up tasty bug treats covered in sap, much like eating a candied apple. If a tree has leaves, the Sapsucker will travel to it, and these birds have been spotted all over the good Earth. Simply look for holes down the trunk of a tree in a straight line— that's this Country Bird's feeding signature.

···• Raisin' a Ruckus •···

Slender in build and shy by nature, the Yellow-billed Cuckoo does in fact have a yellow bill. It has beautiful white spots on the underside of its tail, allowing birders to easily identify this bird correctly, but only if they can spot it. Chowing down on a wide array of caterpillars, this Cuckoo tends to be cutthroat among its household if food is in short supply, and parents are known to "remove" the youngest from the nest to ensure the survival of the other chicks. Sounding more like a repetitive squawk from the Jurassic period, the distinctive call of the Cuckoo helps reveal this elusive Country Bird.

IT'S BEEN REAL NICE

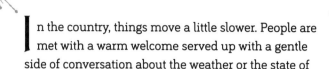

In the country, things move a little slower. People are met with a warm welcome served up with a gentle side of conversation about the weather or the state of the fruit trees in season.

In the country, conversations happen outside on porches or in wide-open spaces bordered by trees that are older than time and flowers that bloom all year-round

In the country, there is no call to hurry. Life is easy. Folks soak in the quiet and still of the afternoon, and there is plenty of time to just *see*.

In the country, folks are charmed immediately by the natural elements all around them, often completely immersed in the chattering of songbirds as the sun rises, or they become lost in colloquial discussions of creatures from one end of an acre to another well past the sun's departure.

In the country, the birds will always welcome you. So don't be a stranger.

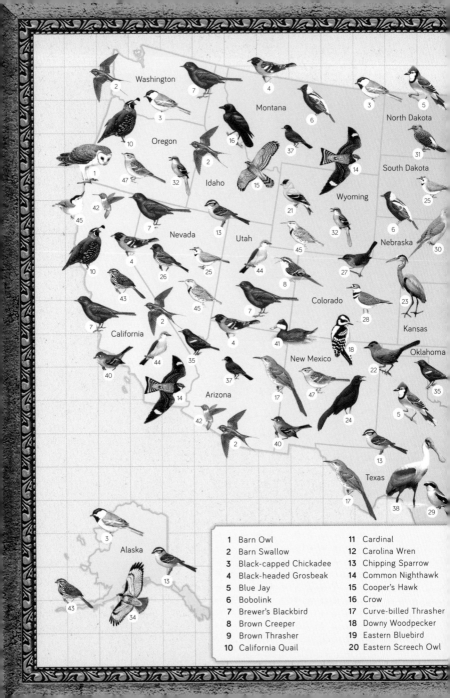

Washington
7
2
3
10
Oregon
1
47
42
45
7
Nevada
10
4
26
43
California
2
7
44
40
35
14
Arizona
42
37
2
40

Montana
4
6
16
37
15
Idaho
2
32
13
Utah
21
45
25
44
8
7
4
41
New Mexico
17
47
24

Wyoming
14
32
27
Colorado
28
18
22
5
13
Texas
17
38

North Dakota
3
5
31
South Dakota
25
6
Nebraska
30
23
Kansas
Oklahoma
35
29

Alaska
3
13
43
34

1	Barn Owl	**11**	Cardinal
2	Barn Swallow	**12**	Carolina Wren
3	Black-capped Chickadee	**13**	Chipping Sparrow
4	Black-headed Grosbeak	**14**	Common Nighthawk
5	Blue Jay	**15**	Cooper's Hawk
6	Bobolink	**16**	Crow
7	Brewer's Blackbird	**17**	Curve-billed Thrasher
8	Brown Creeper	**18**	Downy Woodpecker
9	Brown Thrasher	**19**	Eastern Bluebird
10	California Quail	**20**	Eastern Screech Owl

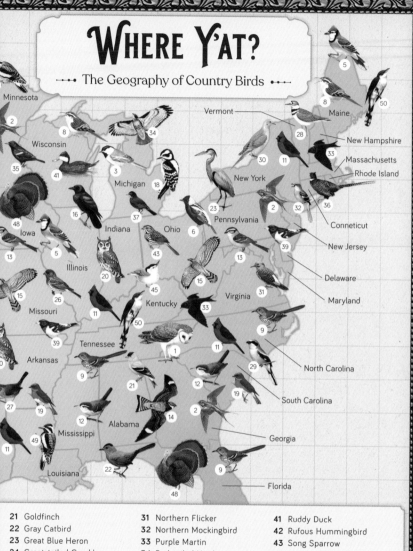

WHERE Y'AT?

→··· The Geography of Country Birds ···←

21	Goldfinch	31	Northern Flicker	41	Ruddy Duck
22	Gray Catbird	32	Northern Mockingbird	42	Rufous Hummingbird
23	Great Blue Heron	33	Purple Martin	43	Song Sparrow
24	Great-tailed Grackle	34	Red-tailed Hawk	44	Western Kingbird
25	Horned Lark	35	Red-winged Blackbird	45	Western Meadowlark
26	House Finch	36	Ring-necked Pheasant	46	White-breasted Nuthatch
27	House Wren	37	Robin	47	White-crowned Sparrow
28	Killdeer	38	Roseate Spoonbill	48	Wild Turkey
29	Loggerhead Shrike	39	Rose-breasted Grosbeak	49	Yellow-bellied Sapsucker
30	Mourning Dove	40	Ruby-crowned Kinglet	50	Yellow-billed Cuckoo

BLESS YOUR HEART

Sayin's & Such

Pretty as the birds we find in the country are the delightful sayings that color the commentary heard by natives to the region. To help those less familiar with the charm of country dialogues, below is a list of common phrases to teach and amuse.

SNAKE
⟶ in the ⟵
GRASS

Someone not to be trusted; best to get a broom

HISSY
FIT

· * ❋ * ·

It is not polite to be mad, so this is used to describe a person angry enough it shows

HAZY
as
COOTER BROWN

Used to describe a person having a hard time standing

FUSSY

Agitated and just plain annoyed

CATTYWAMPUSED

Twisted, turned into all sorts
of positions, and completely
entangled

HIGHFALUTIN

Fancier than rich

DON'T STAND ⊹ a ⊹ CHANCE

All hope is gone

A BIT *much*

A small amount, which
is just too much

Cute as all GET OUT

Adorable every day of the
week, and twice as much
on Sunday

Food is ready for tasting

EYE-CATCHER

Beauty at first glance

GOT GUMPTION

*Tenacious and brave,
with a dash of brazen*

SPITTIN' In The PUNCH BOWL

Spoiled a perfectly good time

FRIENDLINESS IS A SKILL to be D·E·S·I·R·E·D

*Not the sweetest
cookie in the batch*

GUSSIED UP

Dressed to impress!

WORE SLAP OUT

Tired of being tired

THAT DOG WON'T HUNT

There is not a day to come where the idea is ever going to work

HOW THE COW ATE THE CABBAGE

It is a fact, not fiction

EYES IN THE BACK OF YOUR HEAD

Watch for the knife if you turn your back!

LET THE LOCKS *FLY*

Reference to the quintessential Country Mullet that is a business-short haircut in the front with a long haircut party in the back

FANCY

A special occasion

Gettin' FEATHERS RUFFLED

The temperature of one's disposition is rising

ALL GET OUT

Used in place of very, very, or VERY

KNEE-HIGH
⊹ to a ⊹
GRASSHOPPER

Young, tiny, or petite

HEAVENS
to
BETSY

Polite profanity

BLESS
Your
HEART

A disclaimer uttered before telling an ugly truth, necessary to avoid looking unkind

JESUS, TAKE THE WHEEL

Completely unrelated to any religious principle, this describes a situation in which a person just cannot manage what is happening and no longer wants to be in charge

HUSH YOUR MOUTH!

Affectionately said to someone when they need to be quiet

I'll Tell You What

Have you spotted some fascinating feathered friends in the wild?
Make note of all the details on these handy-dandy journaling pages!

Type of Bird

_____

Date | Location

_____

Notes

Type of Bird

_____

Date | Location

_____

Notes

Type of Bird

_____

Date | Location

_____

Notes

Type of Bird

Date | Location

Notes

Type of Bird

Date | Location

Notes

Type of Bird

Date | Location

Notes

Type of Bird

Date | Location

Notes

Type of Bird

Date | Location

Notes

Type of Bird

Date | Location

Notes

Type of Bird

Date | Location

Notes

Type of Bird

Date | Location

Notes

Type of Bird

Date

Location

Notes

Type of Bird

Date

Location

Notes

Type of Bird

Date

Location

Notes

Type of Bird

Date

Location

Notes

Storytellers

Angela Harrison Vinet

A freelance writer for over twenty years, Angela Vinet calls North Louisiana home. As a nature enthusiast, she enjoys any outdoor adventure in her beloved home state. Wife to Robert for more than half her life and mom to three full-of-life boys, Angela stays busy with family outings and baseball practices when she is not writing or teaching school. In her spare time, she enjoys writing children's books, kayaking, and adventuring with her family. Having freelanced for newspapers as a columnist and features writer, her work has appeared in many circulations for local press in addition to the *USA Today* network. Her day job teaching English/Language Arts is quite fulfilling, as she helps children fine-tune their writing skills. As an eternal optimist, Angela lives life to the max, finding the silver linings that life offers while embracing the attitude that kindness toward all things matters as a daily mantra.

Janis Hatten Harrison

Janis is affectionately known throughout the United States as GrandJan. She is a seventy-two-year-old widow who taught herself to drive a camper after her husband's passing. She has since crisscrossed America, camping in her class C RV. GrandJan is an avid birder and has seen many different birds, with up to 580 birds on her life list. Her nemesis bird is the elusive Snowy Owl, but she's confident that she will find it. Making friends wherever she goes, GrandJan has done it all—from playing the washboard in a jug band in the desert to taking drum lessons at age sixty-five. Full of life and fun, GrandJan is always cooking something in the kitchen or working in her garden when she is home. She is currently battling bone cancer and looks forward to getting back to being a full-time GrandJan.

Thank You Kindly

For my parents, who sacrificed many earthly
pleasures so that my sister and I could be more.
To my father, who always believed in me and was
his most proud when he saw my articles in the
newspaper, thank you for never letting me think
I was less. To my mom, who wanted me to become
a strong, independent woman, you never allowed
me to give up on my own dreams. Thank you
for teaching me how to work hard, be
determined, and reach for the stars.
Look, Mom; look, Dad—I made it.
I'm in hardback!

—Angela